D0372977

PRIVATE EYE

Colemanballs

14

A selection of quotes,
most of which originally appeared
in PRIVATE EYE's
'Colemanballs' column.

Our thanks once again to all the readers
who sent us their contributions,
and to whom this book is dedicated.

PRIVATE EYE
Colemanballs
14

Compiled and edited by
BARRY FANTONI

Illustrated by
Bill Tidy

PRIVATE EYE

Published in Great Britain
by Private Eye Productions Ltd,
6 Carlisle Street, London W1D 3BN

© 2008 Pressdram Ltd
ISBN 1 901784 49 7
Designed by Bridget Tisdall
Printed in Great Britain by
Clays Ltd, St Ives plc

Athletics

"Once you've thrown the javelin, it's out of your hands."

TESSA SANDERSON

"Yeah, OK, so I got a personal best – but, for me personally, that just isn't good enough."

JEANETTE KWAKYE

"The Great North Run is the longest half-marathon in the world."

TALKSPORT RADIO

"I wouldn't say he's a one-off, but I think he's an absolute exception."

SIR PHILIP CRAVEN

Boxing

"Fights can be won or lost on the day of the fight."

DAVID HAYE

"He [Ricky Hatton] was unbeaten until he lost."
                                    SIR PETER BLAKE

"Calzaghe has managed to keep all of his
personal problems out of his life"
                                    DUKE McKENZIE

"If Rick Barnhill wins this, it'll be a real scalp in
his cap."
                                    WILL VANDERS

"I've gone from being a global champion to
being a world-wide champion."
                                    RICKY HATTON

Can of Worms

"He [van Persie] is the right player for them – he can open a can of worms."

PAUL MERSON

"And that's a can of worms out of the bottle."

RADIO 5 LIVE

Cricket

"If you want a quiet life you turn a blind ear."

GEOFFREY BOYCOTT

"Bell hangs his head in the air, looking up at the sky."

HENRY BLOFELD

"You're stepping on a treadmill that you don't know where it takes you."

ANDREW STRAUSS

"5-0 is, in fact, a better result for us than the 4-1 on the last tour here."

DUNCAN FLETCHER

"It's the hardest decision I've ever had to make, but also the easiest."

MICHAEL VAUGHAN

"The most important thing about batting is getting the bat to hit the ball."

MICHAEL HOLDING

"The way England capitulated yesterday, it was as if they had given up."

GEOFFREY BOYCOTT

"It would help if the groundsman didn't scatter his seed around the place a couple of days before the match."

JONATHAN AGNEW

"[He] took his bat away posthumously."

HENRY BLOFELD

"Invariably that's what happens. But not always."

ROBIN JACKMAN

"Sometimes your best shot can be your Hercules' heel."

GEOFFREY BOYCOTT

"I think he's going to have to put his head on his heart and tell us he never honestly meant that."

PAUL PARKER

"I'll cross that chestnut when we get to it."

GEOFFREY BOYCOTT

"The Indians will have their reservations about how they have played this."

BRUCE YARDLEY

"We took our finger off the boil..."

DOMINIC CORK

"You go through good troughs, you go through bad troughs."

KEVIN PIETERSEN

"He's like a coiled tiger about to go off like a firecracker."

HENRY BLOFELD

"It's accepted practice for the batsman to get between himself and the fielder..."

TONY GREIG

"I've got broad shoulders, I'll take it on the chin and just get on with it."

STEVE HARMISON

"Andre Nel will not want to get up Sean Tait's end, not with that finger."

SKY SPORTS

"Now it's time to draw a line under the sand..."

PAT MURPHY

"More and more I get asked for my autograph less and less."

DEREK UNDERWOOD

"Andrew Flintoff is to see a renowned joint specialist in Amsterdam."

RADIO 5 LIVE

"It isn't called Windy Wellington just because it rhymes."

GEOFFREY BOYCOTT

"The players want a slice of what is now a huge, huge gravy train..."

JACK BANNISTER

"Everybody is standing behind everyone else."

ROBIN JACKMAN

"The performance in Hamilton was pathetic; there's no other word for it – it was poor."

SIR IAN BOTHAM

"The England bowlers have got a mountain to climb on this flat pitch."

GEOFFREY BOYCOTT

Cycling

"These cyclists are playing chess with each other. They are shuffling the cards even as we speak..."

WORLD CYCLING CHAMPIONSHIPS

"This is the steepest part of the course and I'm afraid it gets steeper later on."

PHIL LIGGETT

Football

"Wenger walks to the edge of his technical area, arms in pockets."

RADIO 5 LIVE

"The umbilical safety cord of the transfer window has been shut."

DOMINIC JOHNSON

"There hasn't been a lot of quality but it's been a high-quality game."

STEVE CLARIDGE

"Celtic's Nakamura hasn't kicked a ball since he came back in anger a fortnight ago."

CHARLIE NICHOLAS

"It was as clear as night is day."

ALAN GREEN

"I'll bet there are eight teams in the last sixteen who won't win the competition."

ANDY GRAY

"...And Hibernian have kicked themselves in the foot..."

ALLAN PRESTON

"It sounds, in many people's eyes, silly."

GRAHAM TAYLOR

"It's time for someone else to take on the mantra."

JIMMY GREAVES

"You can't change a team overnight in a couple of days."

MARTIN O'NEIL

"Berbatov can see things with the outside of his boot."

ALVIN MARTIN

"I'm getting beyond the future now."

ALEX FERGUSON

"Steven Gerrard makes runs into the box better than anyone, so does Frank Lampard."

JAMIE REDKNAPP

"He's the kind of player you only miss when he's not playing."

GRAHAM TAYLOR

"Queen of the South know they've got their tails in front."

MURDO MACLEOD

"Greening, forced to go across the field horizontally."

BBC1

"He was running quicker than his legs could go."

STEVE McCLAREN

"I'm always a little bit disappointed sometimes."

GRAHAM TAYLOR

"Somehow his legs couldn't keep up with the rest of him..."

GLENN ROEDER

"There were lots of examples of poor defending both prior to and preceding the goal."

GARY LINEKER

"...Bournemouth are on a great run and have won their last four games consecutively."

JEFF STELLING

"For Rafa Benitez, the penny has finally sunk in."

GRAHAM BEECROFT

"The way Arsenal are passing the ball is as if they're telepathetic."

GRAHAM TAYLOR

"Football is like a roundabout; sometimes you're up, sometimes you're down."

RADIO 5 LIVE

"Wigan throw a dice into the roulette wheel of the final day of the Premiership."

IVAN GASKELL

"I've always believed at this time of the season you get to see people like oranges – you squeeze them and some of them tend to capitulate."

ADRIAN BOOTHROYD

"I'm at a club where you feel like a spark will get us back on the crest of the wave and help us move up the league – that can give us a platform to build on."

MICHAEL OWEN

"Relieved... anxious... flushed... all the superlatives come out."

STEVE BRUCE

"And Andrew Surman wears his sleeve on his heart for Southampton."

DAVE MERRINGTON

"It's not easy, that's why it's difficult..."

ANDY GRAY

"It is a lot harder when you are 4-1 down than when you are 4-1 up."

KEVIN KEEGAN

"It was a very hot potato at the time. We thought we'd put it to bed, but to have it regurgitated now is pointless."

STEVE COPPELL

"Alonso missed a Champion's League game when his wife was giving birth to his girlfriend."

JASON CUNDY

"Harry Redknapp has had an up-and-down season on and off the pitch but he's had a fantastic season."

ALAN HANSEN

"Well, statistics are there to be broken."

SKY SPORTS

"I don't know if the title is over. It depends on results. In my brain it is not over because mathematically it is never over."

ARSENE WENGER

"And of course this afternoon it's the second half of the Arsenal/Liverpool trilogy…"

TALKSPORT RADIO

"He wants to go back to France... and you can't get nearer to France than Plymouth."

PAUL WALKER

"And I never thought I would say this word – no cutting edge!"

ANDY GRAY

"And he bisected his three attacking players with that cross."

JOHN MOTSON

"The significance of that goal cannot be underestimated."

JOHN MOTSON

"If you came in from the pub and you didn't know who was playing, you wouldn't know who was playing."

NEVILLE SOUTHALL

"What a great one [goal], with his so-called right foot."

DEREK JOHNSTONE

"Everything is being looked at with a fine tooth comb."

GRAEME MURTY

"[Avram] Grant is like a lot of managers – if his team doesn't win tonight he'll be in a no win situation."

GRAHAM TAYLOR

"For the first time, they've been looking again over their shoulder..."

LEE DIXON

"...and Hull City, to use a pun, have really got their tails up."

RADIO LANCASHIRE

"I know they were a non-league team but I definitely did not underestimate them. But it was a surprise that they were so good."

MARTIN SKRTEL

"If there's one thing Derby have lacked this season, it's pace and power."

ALVIN MARTIN

"With apologies to Fred Astaire and Ginger Rogers, will it be Wolves or West Brom who are singing in the rain tonight?"

IAN WINTER

"A tremendous free kick! It probably would have gone in if he had put it where he intended to put it."

STAN COLLYMORE

"Some Hull City supporters have had to wait 104 years for this day."

RADIO 5 LIVE

"He [David Beckham] has lost his legs at the highest level."

CHRIS WADDLE

"Diouf is a master of the dark art of the winger: draws you in, sucks you off..."

GARRY BIRTLES

"There's not many players who would have hit him [Fabio Capello] in the eye and made him put his hat on."

GLENN HODDLE

"Setanta's not just about football. We have the PGA golf and the Scottish Premier League..."

RICHARD BROOKE

"It's like a game of chess now: keep your cards close to your chest."

JASON PRICE

"It's not great on the eyes, but it's super to watch..."

STEVE CLARIDGE

"He dived one-handed like a swan..."

BBC

"He offers something different to what we haven't got."

SIMON GRAYSON

"It's the expected start to this game – Nil-Nil!"

JOHN MURRAY

"He [Wayne Rooney] is inexperienced, but he's experienced in terms of what he's been through."

STEVE McCLAREN

"They [Arsenal] have a lot of games coming up in recent weeks."

LES FERDINAND

"He [Arsene Wenger] selected a team that was stronger than he had available to him."

JOHN ANDERSON

"Chelsea fans will have switched off their televisions and be listening to the radio with their hands over their ears biting their nails."

ALAN GREEN

"The pendulum has swung full circle."

BRYAN HAMILTON

"It could be a right old game of cowboys and soldiers."

MIKE PARRY

"Kevin Keegan is an honest person ... he wears his heart on his chest."

ALAN BRAZIL

"He clearly puts his balls to the hand."

IAIN DOWIE

"Such disappointment etched across the body language of the Carlisle players..."

CONOR McNAMARA

"And Tottenham are fighting like beavers..."

CHRIS KAMARA

"Puyol there at the back; he's the Rock of Gibraltar for Spain."

RAY HUDSON

"You've got to have eyes all over you in a game like this."

GRAHAM TAYLOR

"We're a long way from being where we are."

STEVEN GERRARD

"You can only play against the opposition you play against."

GRAHAM TAYLOR

"I said it pre-season. In fact I may have said it before the season started..."

SIR ALEX FERGUSON

"He's done well against the 'so-called' Chelsea's and Arsenal's..."

STEVE McMANAMAN

"For it to be a tight game, Marseille needed to score first and that never looked likely after Liverpool scored."

DAVID PLEAT

"Gary Neville was captain, and now Ryan Giggs has taken on the mantelpiece."

RIO FERDINAND

"The new West Stand casts a giant shadow over the entire pitch, even on a sunny day."

CHRIS JONES

"If anybody thinks that Juande Ramos can walk in the door at Spurs and do a King Cnut act and turn everything into gold, they are wrong."

GRAHAM HUNTER

"And it's West Ham to start the second half attacking their supporters away to our right..."

RADIO 5 LIVE

"There's not enough expletives to thank the players for what they've done over the course of the season."

JIMMY QUINN

"30 per cent of the black players [in the Premiership] are black..."

PAUL ELLIOT

"We played well and had chances, but then we held a gun to our heads and pulled the trigger twice."

GLENN ROEDER

"Teams relegated will be looking to parachute back up straight away next season."

RONNIE IRANI

"All the shots have been over or above the bar."
STAN COLLYMORE

"Results don't really matter at this level, but you still want to gain a result as that's what it's all about."

EDDIE HOWE

"They are a hard nut to break down."
RAY CLEMENCE

"Paul Jewell's anxiety is written all over his body language."

JOHN MURRAY

"The gods didn't shine on them [Liverpool] last night..."

STEVE McCLAREN

"Tell me about it because you certainly came out with all guns flying!"

DAMIEN JOHNSON

"Yes, injuries are the biggest bed-bug..."

STEVE McCLAREN

"He [the PSV centre half] is like the Tower of Babel in there."

MARK LAWRENSON

"Hennessy has two difficult balls to deal with and he's dealt with them amicably."

KEVIN RATCLIFFE

"I can honestly guarantee that if this game was being played in England it wouldn't take place in this stadium."

TIM VICKERY

"He hit that ball kind of running away from himself."

IAN WRIGHT

"Gordon Strachan is on course to follow Willie Maley and Jock Stein as the only Celtic manager to win three consecutive League titles."

THOMAS McGUIGAN

"He [Crouch] has a very good record of scoring against opposition."

JONATHAN PIERCE

"You need your strikers getting between 19 and 20 goals a season each."

MICKY ADAMS

"He [Cristiano Ronaldo] bears comparison with George Best – the incomparable George Best."

DAVID PLEAT

"It's like he's got velvet gloves on his feet..."

IAN DOWIE

"He [Sir Alex Ferguson] is such a hard worker – even at his age I bet there's no one in before him in the morning and no one leaves earlier than him in the evening."

STEVE BURKINSHAW

"Rafael Benitez is down there making hand signals but no one will hear him in this atmosphere."

MIKE INGHAM

"I suppose that was the sort of game Newcastle fans enjoy – as long as the outcome is what the outcome was at the end of it."

GLENN ROEDER

"I think he was lucky not to be sent off as I've seen players sent off for worse than that."

PETER REID

"He [David Healy] is a big fish in a small fry."

NEIL WARNOCK

"It is a dogfight and when you go into those you have to fight like dogs."

CHRIS COLEMAN

"History is made to be broken."

GERRY FRANCIS

"After that goal, Scotland have the bit between their legs... I mean their tail between their teeth."
BBC

"I'm not saying he's going to field a weaker team; it just won't be as strong."
MARK LAWRENSON

"Middlesbrough have turned the tide of the game on its head."
JONATHAN PIERCE

"Many of them have developed muscles on parts of their bodies that they've never had."
FULHAM FC WEBSITE

"It's a local derby almost every time these two teams meet."

GERRY ARMSTRONG

"He [David Beckham] hasn't spoken much in terms of words in recent weeks."

SKY SPORTS

"I'm 28 now, and they say you peak at 28, so my best years are still ahead of me."

KIERON DYER

"I'm looking forward to anticipating this match."

TALK SPORT RADIO

"He's got two good feet, left and right..."

RONNIE GOODLASS

"Riise's had four chances. I wouldn't say two of them were chances, mind."

ANDY GRAY

"It was a defensive mistake for their goal and it's often goals which decide games."

JIMMY CALDERWOOD

"Riordan can score without a left or a right foot."

ARCHIE McPHERSON

"If they are aware of it, they'll be oblivious of it."

DAVID PLEAT

"Gilardino went down almost posthumously."

ITV SPORT

"I must be a lucky motto."

STEVE CLARIDGE

"Blackburn striker Roque Santa Cruz – a real bargain, if there is such a word."

MATTHEW LORENZO

"Andy Johnson's gone 11 goals without a game..."

NIGEL WINTERBURN

"Fourth spot is what we are aiming for... we don't want to be second best."

PHIL NEVILLE

"It's a game that will ultimately be decided by the final outcome."

MARTIN TYLER

"The scoreline didn't reflect the result..."

MARCUS BUCKLAND

"We can't live in the past – we can only live in the future."

GLENN ROEDER

"I'm better than them at things they can't do..."

JOEY BARTON

"He [Diawara] brings out an extra six to twelve inches and it's a fantastic tackle."

SCOTT MINTO

"He chanced his arm and it came off..."

BRIAN MOORE

"In the second half, Barcelona threw caution to the window."

GARY RICHARDSON

"He [Jose Mourinho] pulls up his trousers as if to say 'a job well done'..."

BBC1

"Even though there are only 400 Andorran supporters here [at Old Trafford], I think that will constitute a record home crowd for them even though they are away from home."

ALAN GREEN

"Baros goes up, Defoe goes up – the only person who doesn't go up is the referee's whistle."

LEE DIXON

"...the defender failed to make a clean fist of the header..."

RADIO WM

"Reading just had a great five-man move that involved everyone..."

PHIL THOMPSON

"...and Gregory Vignal stretches out one of those long left legs of his."

BBC RADIO SOLENT

"... we got back into the game in the second half; unfortunately we failed to turn the nail on them."

STUART PEARCE

"If there's a better goal scored this season, I've yet to see it."

LEE DIXON

"It was a no-win situation for everyone. We knew we had to win, and we did."

STEVE McCLAREN

"You've got to put square pegs in square holes – not the other way round."

STEVE CLARIDGE

"He'll have a pair of sharp and canny shoulders to listen to."

DAVID PLATT

"Glenn Roeder, his arms folded on the bench behind him..."

RADIO 5 LIVE

"We're not as good as we think we are. We need to go out there and prove that."

STEVE McCLAREN

"Both Rafa Benitez and David Moyes have said that they won't be having another number two until the end of the season."

ALAN JACKSON

"I think he made the wrong mistake."

STEVE STONE

"And Stephen Carr is rotating his right kneecap and grimacing."

RADIO NEWCASTLE

"Every game for England is a game for England."

STEVE McCLAREN

"Kuyt can cover the ground better than Crouch, he's got more legs."

CHRIS WADDLE

"We've created a window of opportunity and it's time to walk through that window."

MICKEY ARTHUR

"I'm getting beyond the future now."

ALEX FERGUSON

"...looking over his shoulder as to where he might be going next."

JOHN GREGORY

"When the questions are being asked, that's when you come up with the answers."

ALVIN MARTIN

Golf

"These trees seem to grow every year."

PETER ALLIS

"The 16th – the only hole yesterday that Tiger gave it the big lampooning driver."

KEN BROWN

"Well Padraig [Harrington], on Wednesday you never thought you could defend your title, let alone win it."

SUE BARKER

"Shelagh was right. It was like a dustpan out there yesterday."

BERNARD GALLACHER

"The rain is now coming down vertically, straight into Paul Casey's face."

RADIO 5 LIVE

"It's throwing me in the deep end of the spotlight but we will muddle on."

NICK FALDO

"After all that practice I just need to turn actions into words."

YOUNG GOLFER, SKY SPORTS 2

"It's a lovely evening for watching this entertaining afternoon of golf."

MARK POUGATCH

"I'm a great believer that if you don't get the ball to the hole – it won't go in."

COLIN MONTGOMERIE

Horses

"Later on we'll be talking to Zara Phillips, who won this year's Horse of the Year award."

ANDY TOWNSEND

"I'll be very surprised if there's a surprise result here."

RADIO 5 LIVE AT AINTREE

"I need to pull a rabbit out of the fire here."

JOHN FRANCOME

Literally

"We are in a situation where banks are literally throwing money at us."

JASMINE BIRTLES

"Today is the day Tony Blair steps, quite literally, into the history books."

TOM BRADBY

"Kelly [Sotherton] has the whole crowd here and literally running the 800 metres with her."

COLIN JACKSON

"The heat can quite literally fry your brain like a boiled egg."

ITV4

"The defender was literally – *literally* – up his [Jan Koller's] backside."

ANDY TOWNSEND

"Those pots will literally be going under the hammer in a few moments."

PAUL MARTIN

"It literally tore her apart from within."

'HELLO' MAGAZINE

"The stadium is bouncing, and I mean literally."

PETER DRURY

"David Weir has just scorched past me – literally – to win the wheel chair race."

JOHN INVERDALE

"...the number of dead is literally countless...but runs into tens of thousands."

EVAN DAVIES

"New Zealand threw their wickets away in a desperate show of naivety, and literally handed the advantage to England on a plate."

JONATHAN AGNEW

"...great snooker from Ronnie O'Sullivan – literally just blew Stephen Hendry away."

ANDY TOWNSEND

"I was literally hung out to dry by Tony Blair."

DES SMITH

"When the accident happened in Munich all those years ago, Manchester United was really just on the brink of actually going to the moon, literally."

SIR BOBBY CHARLTON

"The bobsleigh was so fast, it was literally as fast as a bullet out of a gun."

MELINDA MESSENGER

"Under democratically elected governments the people of Pakistan have been literally screwed by their leaders."

RICHARD ARMITAGE

Motor Sport

"Hamilton targeting a podium here this afternoon and already his team-mate Kovalainen is ahead of him in the same car."

JAMES ALLEN

"Lap 41: Trulli pits. More bad luck for Toro Rosso as Vettel trundles out of the race with smoke pouring from his back end."

BBC SPORT WEBSITE

"He [Lewis Hamilton] is an excellent driver, both in and out of the car."

RON DENNIS

"We're back were we want to be, which is behind the top three teams."

NICO ROSBERG

"We're looking for fractions of a second here rather than tenths."

MARTIN BRUNDLE

"I'm not Lewis, but if I were me, I would be furious."

DAMON HILL

"I didn't have any superstitions but I always got in the right side of the car, because I thought it brought me luck."

MARK BLUNDELL

"...any one of two of three men could finish with these, up on the podium this afternoon: Button, Fisichella, Webber, Alonso, Raikkonen."

JAMES ALLEN

"That's the first time I've seen a Haslam on a black Ducati since his father Ron rode a black Norton."

BARRY NUTLEY

Music

"This where he [Haydn] really started nailing his true voice to the mast."

BBC RADIO 3

"I live in my own world. I don't make any apologies for that. I'm sorry if it offends anyone."

LEO SAYER

"Brahms only wrote three string quartets in his lifetime."

SARA MOHR-PIETSCH

"He [Tony Wilson] understood that history is made, in a way, by those who make it."

PAUL MORLEY

"There's always going to be a few bad eggs in a barrel."

ROGER DALTREY

"After the break, we will play something from one of the best 70s albums of all time."

NICK FRANCIS

Oddballs

"I've had one of the worst upbringings of my life."

GUEST ON JEREMY KYLE PROGRAM

"The man who killed Jill Dando wins his appeal against his conviction..."

PETER LEVY

"Not bad, but not what you need to do when you're trying to do what you need to do..."

NBC (US)

"I'm looking at an empty cattle market. About a week ago this would have been full of 20,000 sheep, and this morning there's not a sausage to be seen..."

NATASHA PEACH

"It's so hot today you could crack a boiled egg on the pavement and cook it."

DAVID ROTHWELL

"My parents were Victorian. They were from the war generation."

RHONA CAMERON

"The Coen brothers are a one-man band."

RADIO 4

"Barbados, an island completely surrounded by water..."

SKY SPORTS 1

"We operate 24/7, six days a week."

RADIO 4

"They have not thought the whole picture through."

PROFESSOR ROBIN LOVELL-BADGE

"It's one of those stories, whatever you think about it, you think something about it."

SUSANNAH STREETER

"He [Lucian Freud] is a living artist, so you could say he's not even dead yet."

ANDREA CATHERWOOD

"The council will probably draw a blind eye over it."

BBC1

"We flew in by air..."

KAREN ALLEN

"They've found a chink in the jigsaw..."

DR HILLARY JONES

"The number of Britons on anti-depressants has hit an all-time high."

KIRSTY WALKER

"Because the Bishop of Harare would not condemn homosexuals he is facing rearguard action."

PETER BYLES

"Cheap cider's a hot potato..."

RUSSELL FULLER

"Because Heather Mills has a prosthetic leg I think she has a lot of support."

GMTV

"He has lived here for at least the whole of his life."

TRUDI BARKER

"One of the stores has 6000 square feet
dedicated to shoes."

DENNIS MURRAY

"...no, it's so invisible you can't see it..."

KATIE PRICE

"You're under arrest for resisting arrest."

POLICEMAN

"I feel we're at the very precipice of a runaway train."

RADIO 4

"Since last year we've raised the goalposts."

CHRISTINE GILBERT

"Is that relevant or are we just barking up a red herring kind of tree?"

VICTORIA DERBYSHIRE

"Over one hundred endangered species are in danger."

AASMAH MIR

"It's hard to pin your finger on what went wrong."

2BR RADIO

"My father introduced me to the world of literacy."

GERI HALLIWELL

"...he was nearly a victim of his own demise."

ADAM BAKER

"We've all lost it, but there's losing it and there's losing it – and that's the latter."

RICHARD BACON

"With hindsight, what has happened is utterly predictable."

CHRIS WOODHEAD

"The kangaroos are sitting ducks."

BBC RADIO 4

"...only 11 percent of female clinical academics are women..."

JANE DACRE

"You could argue, the British sense of humour is unique to Britain."

GENERAL SIR MICHAEL JACKSON

"...poverty is a movable feast."

KELVIN MACKENZIE

"Police in South Wales have asked residents to leave their homes in a caravan park."

RADIO 5 LIVE

"You shouldn't expect her to run after you with her head in the sand".

JEREMY KYLE

"There was Damien Hirst standing next to this decapitated head."

TRACEY EMIN

"We will be inviting survivors and their families, and the victims [of the Manchester United Munich air crash] and their families."

DAVID GILL

"The world's tallest man got married today in China, after a search for a bride that stretched around the world."

BBC RADIO 4

"During the war we had ARPs which stands for 'Air Raid Wardens'."

RADIO TAY

"Some parents buy double beds for their 15-year-olds and encourage all comers."

BBC RADIO 4

"The mathematicians have got their calculuses out."

ALISTAIR HIGNELL

"There's more secrets in my family than there is in a hot dinner."

JEREMY KYLE

"There is fog on the A417 between Cirencester and Birdlip – that's both ways."

SEVERN SOUND

"Welcome to our early morning soiree..."

PETE MITCHELL

"This helicopter is unique, it is one of only two in the country."

BBC POINTS WEST

"If you're one of the 40,000 people without power this evening..."

BBC2

"A lot of time's gone under the bridge since then."

MARK LAMARR

"Blue skies all over the country from dusk to dawn."

BBC RADIO 4

"Bob Monkhouse has done a terrific job since he died."

PAUL MILLER

"We felt we needed an umbrella organisation to help flood victims."

MARY DHONAU

"In the future, I plan on taking more of an active role in the decisions I make."

PARIS HILTON

"There is a digital radio station dedicated to the birdsong; it's doing very well, if it's still going."

JOHN HUMPHRYS

"That was such an educational shoot ... it learned me so much."
CONTESTANT, BRITAIN'S NEXT TOP MODEL

"...they discovered that helicopter pilots' first reaction when they have any problem at all is to drop their load."
BBC RADIO 4

"Her biggest scalp since she gave birth in June last year..."
EUROSPORT

"He [Max Mosley] is not taking this lying down."
SKY NEWS

"A blind man was attacked by two men, one believed to be a woman."
PETER LEVY

"And take care if you are visiting family or relatives."
DEBBY LINLEY

Politics

"Every major green thing that's been done in our history, from cleaning the water under Disraeli to cleaning the air under Harold Macmillan, has been done by a Tory government."

JOHN GUMMER

"We are going to get on top of this and get to the bottom of it."

CONDOLEEZZA RICE

"He'll be haunted by that, not for the rest of his life, but until the day he dies."

ALEX SALMOND

"In the Budget, that rabbit pulled from the hat backfired."

NORMAN SMITH

"Adam Crozier is throwing things into the fire to upset the applecart."

ROYAL MAIL STRIKER

"Most of the faith schools we've got already exist."

LADY ESTELLE MORRIS

"The hypocrisy is on the other foot..."

PHIL WOOLAS

ETHEL FRIGGS
HYPOCHIROPODIST

"You don't make oysters without some sand to begin with."

FRANK FIELD

"Dispatches lifts the lid on New Labour – The Blunkett Tapes – from the man who saw it all."

CHANNEL 4

"I don't have a benchmark – the benchmark is the next election."

DAVID CAMERON

"The glue that is holding New Labour together is coming apart at the seams."

JAMES LANSDALE

"Keep vigilant, watch the local radio."
BARONESS YOUNG

"You don't have to be a Christian to believe that we are all created in God's image."
EDWARD LEIGH

"Once MPs have left the chamber following Prime Minister's Questions, Jacqui Smith, the Home Secretary, can start on cannabis."
BBC NEWS

"Jon Cruddas has joined the ever-increasing set of horses who are throwing in their hats for the race to become deputy leader of the Labour Party."

JAMES LANDALE

"When we're doing well we all enjoy the wind our colleagues produce."

JACK STRAW

"There's no alternatives from David Cameron to the big answers that Gordon Brown's providing solutions for."

PETER HAIN

"However she [Hillary Clinton] cuts the cake, she has a huge mountain to climb."

JAMES KUMRASARMI

"His bulimia was private grief of a workaholic with too much on his plate."

MICHAEL WHITE

"This is all about historical events in the past."

TONY BLAIR

Question & Answer

Q: Favourite item of clothing?

A: My watch. I got it for my birthday and I haven't had it off since.

SHAUN MURPHY

PAUL O'GRADY: Do you have any superstitions?

ANNA REID: I don't have any superstitions. I deliberately do everything differently every night before I go on.

CHANNEL 4

JANE OMOROGBE: You had an advantage tonight Charles, because Nils said he had never played you before.

CHARLES LOSPER: Well, it works both ways because I have never played him either.

ITV1

Royals

"About this time, King Abdullah is getting an official reception, and a little bit of heckling, from the Queen..."

STEVE WRIGHT

"The two things are exactly similar."

DUCHESS OF YORK

"Prince Harry will be the first member of the Royal Family to serve in Iraq since his uncle Prince Andrew fought in the Falklands in 1982."

RADIO 5 LIVE

Rowing

"Cambridge have won the Boat Race. Oxford were second."

GEOFF TWENTYMAN

Rugby

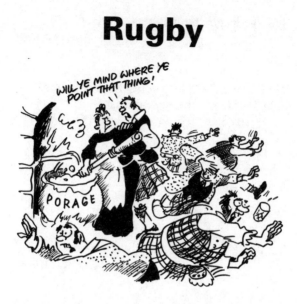

"They [Scotland] are staring down the barrel of a wooden spoon."

WILL GREENWOOD

"At the end of the day, we're going home tomorrow..."

NEW ZEALAND STUDIO GUEST, ITV

"It's a very responsible job, so there is a huge amount of responsibility."

MARTIN JOHNSON

"It's like Rugby by numbers... A, B, C..."
                                                    DEWI MORRIS

"He [Gerald Davis] was only a small man so I
looked up to him because of that."
                                                    SHANE WILLIAMS

"The team played better in the second half than
they are capable of."
                                                    NEWSTALK 106 RADIO

"Look at the three of them, working in tandem."
                                                    DEWI MORRIS

"It goes without saying that the egg timer is
slipping away."
                                                    JOHN INVERDALE

"Obviously the changing room's full of ecstasy
and everybody's happy..."
                                                    LAWRENCE DALLAGLIO

"Inevitably there's going to be a lot of wailing of
teeth in the newspapers tomorrow."
                                                    JOHN INVERDALE

"It's easier to play rugby without the ball in this game."

DAVID SOLE

"He [Farrell] is made of steel and has the broken nose to prove it."

SONIA MACLOUGHLAN

"He leapt like an eagle."

BRIAN NOBLE

"Fiji make the simple things look easy."

JOHN BEATTIE

"They've got their tails up now because their noses are in front."

GREGOR TOWNSEND

"Every [Fifian] point is a hammer in the Welsh coffin."

WILL GREENWOOD

"GPW have been long-time supporters of the Saints and we're sure this partnership will have a platitude of benefits for both organisations."

TONY COLQUITT

"The rain was coming down sideways."

MIKE BLAIR

"He was only a small man so I looked up to him because of that".

SHANE WILLIAMS

"A lot of these players can't cope without discipline. It's like Pavlova's dog out there."

IEUAN EVANS

"16 stone stand-off; you don't see many of those on a dark street."

BBC1

"Now for a birds eye view, let's go down to the touchline..."

NICK MULLINS

Snooker

"Ronnie is one of the greatest ever players but he is going to have to win some more competitions before he will be considered one of the greatest ever."

JOHN VIRGO

"He [Ding] was in tears. Ronnie O'Sullivan put his arm around him and cajoled him."

PRESENTER, TALKSPORT

"John Higgins would know that if the cue was on the other foot he'd expect his opponent to play to win."

JOHN VIRGO

"It's like Stevie's holding a tiger by the tail, and Ronnie can't wait to get amongst the balls."

JOHN PARROTT

"Day has missed balls this evening that he never misses."

CLIVE EVERTON

"Ken Doherty needs to win the next two frames... a huge probability but highly unlikely."

WILLIE THORNE

"If the red wasn't where it was, he couldn't have played that shot."

WILLIE THORNE

"It's hard to describe, it's very disappointing. I didn't play like I can and to drop out of the top 16 is the icing on the cake."

KEN DOHERTY

"He's second favourite for this frame..."

TERRY GRIFFITHS

"There was plenty of brown poking out; it must have been the tension."

JOHN VIRGO

"Somebody like John Higgins who was the current World Champion."

JOHN PARROTT

"If you played this 100 times, you'd pot it 99.9."

WILLIE THORNE

"He's missed more balls than he's gone for!"

JOHN VIRGO

"He [John Parrot] has jumped out of his chair like a greyhound."

JOHN VIRGO

"When he gets among the balls he does the lemming thing like a kamikaze pilot and falls on his sword."

STEVE DAVIS

Swimming

"Hopefully, by next year our swimmers will be competing on a level playing field."

BBC MIDLANDS TODAY

Tennis

"My shoulder is not where I want it to be... but I've done a good job of monitoring it."

MARIA SHARAPOVA

"He [Tim Henman] is one of the world's best returners in terms of getting the ball back."

JOHN LLOYD

"A win is a win... except of course when it's not a win, then it's not a win."

VENUS WILLIAMS

"Nadal tried to hit Tsonga in the nuts with that ball but somehow he managed to get some wood on it."

JEFF TARANGO

"...you've gotta say that. It goes without saying."

JOHN McENROE

"Andy Murray: the last British man in the men's or women's draw."

JOHN INVERDALE

"Laura Robson – solid between the ears."

VIRGINIA WADE

"Her father Richard likens her [Venus Williams] to a gazelle, bounding around the court, and there she is pouncing on her prey."

RADIO 5 LIVE

"I sort of believe that he can win every match that he plays, and therefore if that's the case, then he's got a chance."

TIM HENMAN

"So Andy Murray reaches his first Masters final. Now that is real consistency."

BBC NEWS

"He's [Federer] been the best player for many years to come."

JOHN LLOYD

"Here's hoping he can force some unforced errors."

TIM HENMAN

"...three times a quarter finalist, he's played at the highest level."

ANDREW CASTLE